The Story of Greatville

The Story of Greatville

a rhymed history fable

by Mark Ensomme
illustrated by Jason Velazquez

LIBERTY HILL PUBLISHING

Liberty Hill Publishing
2301 Lucien Way #415
Maitland, FL 32751
407.339.4217
www.libertyhillpublishing.com

Illustrated by: Jason Velazquez

Thank you to The Atlas Society for assisting with editing and collaborating with me on this book.

Paperback ISBN-13: 978-1-66287-981-4
Hard Cover ISBN-13: 978-1-66287-982-1
Ebook ISBN-13: 978-1-66287-983-8

To Kylee and Ayden

May you always enjoy the
blessings of liberty.

"History never repeats itself,
but it does often rhyme."

-Mark Twain

The story of Greatville
goes back a long way,
back to a different
and far-removed day.

It begins in the days
before Greatville was found,
before there was anyone
to walk Greatville ground.

Back before Greatville,
and its life-changing things,
the world that existed
was ruled by the kings.

They ruled by the notion
that the one was not vital,
that the needs of the many
held ultimate title.

And under this theory
of "good for the all,"
the rights of the one
were ever so small.

From all the crops raised
the kings took a share,
using soldiers and armies
and calling it "fair."

From every pie baked
the kings took a slice,
claiming life in the kingdoms
required this "price."

And above all their subjects,
the kings lived in splendor,
enjoying the spoils
that their rules did engender.

They restricted all thoughts,
restrained what was said,
controlled who went hungry,
said who got what bread.

They ruled by brute force,
through the power of might,
inverting the concepts,
of wrong and of right.

And just what this led to,
we know from the lore,
was a world of despair,
of gloom and hard chore.

Discomfort and lacking,
poverty and pain,
nights with no shelter
in the cold and the rain.

Sickness and wanting,
hardships and woe,
long days of hard labor,
with nothing to show.

Lives that were short,
filled with darkness at night,
sweat in the summers,
and not much delight.

Yes, this was the world
when the kings had their way,
when force and compulsion
ruled the day.

Then one renowned day,
before Greatville was known,
a new land was spotted,
in a hard-to-reach zone.

This new land was spacious,
with fields wide and vast,
and news of this treasure,
began to spread fast.

A few saw this land,
as a way to start new,
as a way to make changes,
so long overdue.

"Let's make it different,"
these hopeful souls cried.
"Let's take the world forward,
in one great big stride!

"Let's acknowledge those rights,
overlooked in the past,
the rights of the one,
as the first, not the last.

Let's make these rights basic,
to all we enact,
let's ensure that the one's rights,
are firmly intact.

"Let's form a safe haven,
where all folks are free,
where you can be yourself,
and I can be me.

"Let's make it a place,
that gives all a fair chance,
where one's own best efforts,
control one's advance.

"Let's make it a place,
where one's gains are retained,
where the rights of possession,
are strictly maintained.

"Let's make it a place,
where the ones have the say,
where only from the ones,
can the state have its way."

So right then and there,
in this newly found land,
Greatville's founders decided
to take up a stand.

A stand against rulers,
takings and tolls,
a stand against kings
controlling their souls.

A stand against bans
on what they could say.
A stand against rulers
who got in the way.

A stand against judgments
without any cause.
A stand against evil
and unrighteous laws.

So, stand they sure did
to defy would-be kings.
They stood with the courage
that righteousness brings.

They took up brave stands
against things that were wrong.
They took stands despite powers
of kings still so strong.

And after much struggle,
much valor and sweat,
the founders of Greatville
dispelled the king threat.

They'd fought and they'd won,
overcoming great odds,
thus shedding the shackles
of any would-be king gods.

And once they had won,
and the kings' rule was past,
they resolved, then and there,
to make their stand last.

They resolved to pass on
the liberty they'd gained,
by setting down guidelines
with freedoms ingrained.

So they wrote Greatville's Guidelines
with these things in mind,
they wrote Greatville's Guidelines
for all humankind.

The Guidelines were rigid,
well-stated, and clear;
they gave Greatville a heading
upon which to steer.

The Guidelines set limits
on those who would lead;
they spelled out restrictions
for leaders to heed.

The Guidelines made clear
that authority must be small
in order for freedoms
to remain standing tall.

The Guidelines gave liberty
to each and every one,
and spoke that these blessings
must not be undone.

And so, with this heading,
Greatville was started,
and out of ideals
a new course was charted.

Greatville was first,
in the history of nations,
to recognize one's rights
at its very foundations.

Greatville was first
to start with a code,
a code based in reason,
with tenets that showed.

And the founders of Greatville
were not disappointed,
as a miracle erupted
from what they'd anointed.

People in old lands
from the Guidelines found cheer,
as a way to escape from
the king lands of fear.

So to Greatville they fled
in pursuit of their dreams.
They came in great numbers,
they came in great streams.

They trekked from the tropics,
they paddled from the poles,
they hiked from the hilltops,
they hopped from their holes.

They sailed from the islands,
they paraded from the plains,
they rowed from the lands
of the downpouring rains.

The blue hairs, the red hairs,
the no hairs at all,
everyone came,
from the big to the small.

And though they were different,
and not all the same,
they all became villagers
in both heart and in name.

And the Greatville they flocked to,
and the land so regarded,
was a land based on rights,
in the past so discarded.

The Guidelines in Greatville
gave great cause for hope;
they were brilliant in vision
and broad in their scope.

In Greatville each villager
was the one in control
of their work and their home,
and their life, and their soul.

Red, white, or blue hair,
the shade didn't matter;
the Guidelines gave all folks
a try on life's ladder.

By the Guidelines all rulers
were kept at a distance
from meddling with merchants
or in matters of subsistence.

And just what this led to
was wondrous to see,
as the progress was something
of unheard-of degree.

Without the kings' takings,
there was newfound incentive
to be more ambitious,
adept and inventive.

Now fueled by the yearning
to improve their own station,
the villagers produced masses
of fresh innovation.

They designed all new tools,
new machines and devices,
new gadgets and levers,
and even new spices.

New plows for the fields,
new belts for the barns,
new wheels for weaving,
and spinning new yarns.

New pulleys for plowing,
planting and picking,
new grease for the gadgets
to keep them all ticking.

New toys for the home,
new saws for the shop,
new seeds that extended
the size of the crop.

New food-freezing freighters,
new far-reaching haulers,
new ready-made dinners,
new long-range home callers.

New instant hot cookers,
new cold cuisine keepers,
new sounds that surrounded,
and clear-vision peepers.

New push-button lamps,
new horseless go-getters,
new dirty-clothes cleaners,
and paperless letters.

All over Greatville
new wonders appeared,
results of the progress
this free land endeared.

Now with all these new blessings
to make old tasks lighter,
the people of Greatville
had futures much brighter.

Now, unlike in old times
when life had been short,
the villagers found free time
for leisure and sport.

Leisures like picnics,
and trips to the shore,
ball games and concerts,
where spirits could soar.

Dinners with laughter,
dances and games,
cookout celebrations,
and sky-lighting flames.

Life became better,
became filled with new perks,
as the villagers found value
in each other's works.

They found worth in owning
the things others made,
in giving and getting
through unhindered trade.

They found worth in working
to make others pleased,
in seeing their own needs
by such work appeased.

And so, from this fountain,
all the villagers became richer,
and everyone gained
in the really big picture.

Prices went down
as merchants competed
to sell to the villagers
the things they all needed.

Misuse and wasting
was in Greatville curtailed,
as ways most efficient
were the ways that prevailed.

Greatville's stores became known
for their troves of fresh treasures,
as merchants tried harder
to bring people pleasures.

And since nothing but free will
compelled anyone to act,
fairness and justice
were firmly intact.

In Greatville, good nature
and peace were the norm,
as free trade and riches
swept the land like a storm.

The merchants, the bankers,
the farmers and growers,
the bakers and doctors,
and newspaper throwers,

The fixers, the florists,
the fryers and flippers,
the sailors and sawyers,
the long-way fast shippers,

Villagers all over
respected their neighbors
in a land where successes
matched efforts and labors.

A villager was someone
with pride and with hope,
with faith in themself
to find ways to cope.

In Greatville a value
was placed on one's deeds,
not on the scope
of misfortune or needs.

Free choice was the key,
deeds really mattered,
force and compulsion
were evils thus shattered.

So Greatville kept growing,
kept reaching new heights,
like an anthem to the wonderful
virtues of rights.

Soon Greatville became
the model of nations,
the font of goodwill
of wealth and creations.

Greatville was proof
for the whole world to see,
proof of the greatness
that mankind could be.

But despite all the happiness,
despite all the pride,
despite the move forward
in one great big stride,

Despite all these things
and the greatness of their land,
some villagers themselves
began finding fault with their hand.

They began to take pleasures
and comforts for granted,
they forgot that all harvests
once had to be planted.

They forgot that all progress
was a product of the mind;
they dismissed all the efforts
behind each new find.

They began to take issue
with those who earned more;
they began to seek riches
without all the chore.

Some grew slothful and lazy
and soon sought the unearned,
and they called for achievers
to somehow be spurned.

They forgot how their Guidelines,
and the Greatville foundation,
had inspired the growth,
the wealth, and creation.

They forgot that in Greatville
free choice ruled all trade,
that choices determined
when fortunes were made.

They forgot that in Greatville
life was better than before,
That her people lived longer,
That her people had more.

And last, but not least,
for this was the worst,
they forgot that in Greatville
the one's rights came first!

So they began to seek edicts
by which they could glean
the things they could not earn
by fair and just means.

And this gleaning by statute
is just what Greatville saw,
as Sneaks Wanting Power
began exploiting this flaw.

Sneaks Wanting Power
craved old king-like might
and labeled Greatville's freedoms
as things to indict.

Sneaks Wanting Power
told folks with smaller portions
that Greatville's free trade
should be blamed for "distortions."

Sneaks Wanting Power
claimed the prosperous had cheated,
then proclaimed the successful
must now be defeated.

Sneaks Wanting Power
stressed envy and classes,
as they stirred up the fears
and the greed of the masses.

They dreamed up new handouts,
new fear seeds to sow,
new problems to fix,
new favors to bestow.

They dreamed up protections
from dangers not present,
they gave solemn pledges
they'd make life more pleasant.

And with all these new favors,
and "wrongs" to make right,
Sneaks Wanting Power
gained old king-like might.

They formed Greatville Central
and called it GC,
a place for the Sneaky
to govern the free.

In time they filled GC
with buildings so vast,
that to be there and see it
left some folks aghast.

They filled these huge structures
with planners and pillagers,
whom they tasked with directing
the lives of the villagers.

And in time there were planners
for farmers and fuels.
There were planners for swamps,
for sculptures and schools.

There were planners for oceans,
for animals and wheat;
there were even strategists
for what villagers should eat!

There were planners for planners,
and more planners for those;
there were Sneaks Wanting Power
paid just to suppose.

And in time there were edicts
on barter and trade;
there were limits on wages
the villagers were paid.

They controlled rents and fares
and all kinds of prices;
they made up strict rules
for all new devices.

Pulleys for picking
could only stretch twenty yards,
and could not be turned on
without six safety guards.

Merchants on mountains
had to hire from the plains,
even if the wage paid
was more than the gains.

Flippers could not flip
without a Sneak's safety blessing
and three months of lessons
on flip-landing guessing.

Trading, once free,
with this growth became guided
by those in GC
and what they decided.

Having pull became better
than pulling one's weight,
and those with the pull
became Greatville's new "great."

Restrictions on wages
made many jobs rarer,
as merchants resisted
this force to be "fairer."

New statutes on tools
made some supplies short,
as decreasing profits
slowed merchant support.

Edicts on fuels
made crop prices rise,
as growers passed on
this "good for all" prize.

And the Sneaks brought back takings
from all villagers employed,
to give coupons and prizes
which some sure enjoyed.

Goodies then free
saw a much-increased use,
as these new unearned handouts
encouraged abuse.

In time Greatville had thousands
of villagers on the dole,
deprived of all purpose,
vision, or goal.

And for those who did work,
the takings kept growing,
leaving less of their earnings
there for the showing.

They lost in large portions
to the Sneaks in Power Central;
they had their funds pilfered
for "just the essential."

And the merchants of Greatville,
on whose backs she was built,
were labeled as bad guys
and shouldered with guilt.

They were chastised and punished,
and told they must pay;
they were used as the fodder
which the Sneaks used as prey.

And in the new Greatville
of contempt for the able,
the people soon wondered
what went wrong with their fable?

They wondered why two workers
brought home what once just took one,
back in the old days
before the change was begun.

They wondered why so many shops
often shut down or closed,
leaving the craftsmen
unemployed and opposed.

They wondered why more work
left them less to retain,
as Sneak Central's takings
caused more and more strain.

They wondered why aged folks
had less time for tots,
while Sneak Central's takings
took more from their pots.

They wondered why young folks
saw taking and stealing
as ways to fill wishes
without a guilt feeling.

They wondered why many villagers
so often stopped caring,
why their hearts were so hardened
by this forced-upon sharing.

They wondered why Greatville,
which once was so strong,
seemed to be crumbling
with so much gone wrong.

They wondered and wondered,
as if with no clue,
why they had problems
or what they should do.

So they called a great council,
and invited all Greatville's "brains,"
to come to Sneak Central
to solve Greatville's pains.

They called all the thinkers,
invited all the "elite,"
to come to this council
for this big brain-trust meet.

So come they all did,
from all different factions,
they came to Sneak Central
to talk about actions.

The blue hairs sent their guy,
and the reds sent their own,
The haulers sent hailers,
to make their needs known.

The white hairs sent two shills,
to be sure they weren't missed,
for the white hairs had plenty
of needs on their list.

The bakers were there,
they even brought a baked feast
in the hopes that their bread price
would soon be increased.

Every single subgroup,
of every zone, job, and size,
sent someone to council
to seek some new prize.

There was much to be gained
from the council's decisions,
and each group had wish lists,
demands, and big visions.

So, the council began,
amid hordes of attention,
from subgroups in Greatville,
too many to mention.

And with all of the voices
competing in this din,
no one in Greatville
was sure what they'd win.

So they watched with great interest
as the council began,
as shill after shill
proposed some new plan.

Some plans were well-liked,
while others were hated;
for days in Sneak Central
the "great minds" debated.

They went round and round,
they raved and they ranted,
they lobbied and argued,
struck deals and recanted.

They stayed there for weeks,
giving speech after speech,
each speaking of something
that seemed good to reach.

But what was good for the red hairs
was often bad for the blue,
or took from the white hairs,
which caused them to stew.

And the growers and shippers,
who before had struck deals,
spent two weeks in squabbles
about fair rate appeals.

And the bread price for bakers,
which to them made such sense,
meant to bread users
more food cost expense.

So on the thing went,
as days turned to weeks,
as plan after plan
brought endless critiques.

They could not make headway,
could not find common ground,
at Greatville's big council,
so "highly" renowned.

Until finally one day,
on day seventy-six,
in walked a young villager
into the mix.

Her name was Arynnda,
a lass so petite
that every head turned
as she joined the "elite."

They all stopped their chatter,
and they all turned to stare
at this villager so junior
to all of them there.

She was small by all measures,
even for a child,
and her eyes glowed like embers
with a fire that seemed wild.

There was life in her eyes,
and all around this young lass
could be seen the old spirit
of true Greatville sass.

And the lass was undaunted
as she entered the hall,
as she strode to the platform
in front of them all.

She stepped on a codebook,
shrugged and cleared her young throat,
and she began an oration
which made all take note.

She said, "My name is Arynnda,
and I've watched your debates,
I've watched your attempts
to decide Greatville's fates.

"You've come to this capital
to try to make choices,
to try to make plans
that please all of our voices.

"You each have a vision
of what Greatville should be,
of what would be best
in this land of the free.

"But what you all miss,
in this frenzy of choosing,
is how choice is tainted,
and what we are losing.

"For freedom is fragile
and will surely fade fast,
unless our great nation
can learn from its past.

"Our land became great
when the kings were unseated,
when force and compulsion
were back then defeated.

"Our Guidelines were simple,
they did not leave a doubt;
They spelled out the dangers
of centralized clout.

"But every citizen here
would let these rules wane,
if they thought that somehow
their own group would gain.

"You've come here to clamor
for perks for your set,
ignoring the costs
of the things that you get.

"You ignore what is lost
when you gain some new favor,
you ignore how our Guidelines
will be forced to waver.

"You forget what goes around
comes around, too.
That one day your own rights
will be but a few.

"For no plan proposed
ever works like is claimed,
and always, yet always,
a new plan is named.

"Like lambs to the slaughter,
you propose ever more
to fix the disasters
of the plans from before.

"And every new plan,
no matter the goal,
brings with it to Greatville
some form of control.

"And every control
has some form of cost,
in freedoms and choices
and rights that are lost.

"And today I see all of you
abandoning rights,
in search of more coupons,
perks and delights.

"You think things are free
when provided by these Sneaks,
who take from your efforts
with their self-righteous shrieks.

"You tolerate the taxes,
the levies and bills,
while the Sneaks Holding Power
reap from the tills.

"You look to this stronghold
to fix your own failings,
and you cry for more handouts
in pitiful wailings.

"But solutions won't come
from any Sneaks in a tower;
it is we who are living
who hold the real power.

"Solutions don't come
from any would-be kings here,
They lie in the freedoms
you once did revere.

"With all of your differences,
you red, white, and blue,
why should Sneaks in this capital
decide things for you?

"And why should all villagers
pay more for their bread,
because someone with power
was at this feast fed?

"Why should you all
not work things out on your own,
instead of losing choices
to those here on the throne?

"You all are adults
and should be treated as such.
You don't need this leviathan
and its Sneaks out of touch.

"You don't need more rules,
more orders and guidance,
you don't need these handouts
with their rules for compliance.

"You don't need this capital,
and all its excuses,
its waste and corruption,
its fraud and abuses.

"You do not need this monster
with its Sneaks on the take;
what you need is more freedom
to keep what you make.

"You don't need this titan,
and its 'good for all' end,
which force our great Guidelines
to break and to bend.

"What you need at this council,
of squabbles unending,
is a shill for those rights
most in need of defending.

"What you need in this nation,
with so much to gain,
is an all-out uproarious
one's rights campaign.

"This campaign must see all folks
take stands and stand strong
against the new king threat
once seen as so wrong.

"This campaign must see all of us,
become the crusaders,
for workers and merchants,
and the rights of all traders.

"And if we with convictions,
can do all these things,
can take away power,
from Greatville's new kings.

"If we can do this,
as was done in our past,
this land we call Greatville,
may yet for long last."

And with that Arynnda stopped,
raised her head and stepped down,
leaving them silent,
in that gigantic town.

The shills were left speechless,
red-faced with shame,
each knowing that their deeds,
took some of the blame.

And the Sneaks in the capital,
who yet yearned to be kings,
stammered and stuttered,
in light of these things.

And villagers all over,
saw the truth and took heart,
for they saw that their actions,
had nearly torn them apart.

For the truth that was spoken,
from the mouth of this child,
made clear to those hearing,
that they all had gone wild.

The truth was so simple,
so easy to see,
the people themselves
were the ones who were key.

So from Arynnda was reborn
the hope that had died,
the brave Greatville spirit,
the distinct Greatville pride.

And that is the ending,
of this based-in-truth fable
about hope and freedom
and Arynnda so able.

So if you are a villager,
or have held Greatville's dream,
if one's rights to you
reign high and supreme.

If you have what that lass had,
that strong Greatville will,
that I believe lives on
in some people still,

Speak out like you mean it,
speak out above the chatter,
don't forget that your one voice
truly does matter.

Speak out like young Arynnda,
find your one special way,
for Greatville is your land,
at least for today.

This story was written in the hope that the ideals set forth by America's Founding Fathers will forever continue to bless the lives of people everywhere.

"The smallest minority on earth is the individual. Those who deny individual rights cannot claim to be defenders of minorities."
Ayn Rand

"It is capitalism that has made possible the enormous advances not only in providing the necessities and amenities of life, but in science, technology, and knowledge of all kinds, upon which civilization rests." Henry Hazlitt

"The Constitution cannot protect us unless we protect the Constitution." Thomas Sowell

"Our cause is the cause of all mankind...we are fighting for their liberty in defending our own." Benjamin Franklin

"The United States of America is the greatest, the noblest, and, in its original founding principles, the only moral country in the history of the world." Ayn Rand

"For everything that is really great and inspiring is created by the individual who can labour in freedom." Albert Einstein

"Each time a man stands up for an ideal, or acts to improve the lot of others, or strikes out against injustice, he sends forth a tiny ripple of hope." Robert F. Kennedy

A note to readers, young and old alike

Thank you for taking the time to read this story. It was written for everyone who cares about the ideals expressed within and wishes to share them with the people around them. Ours is a country of speaking out, sharing ideas, and improving the world through our own individual quests to improve our own lives. Each of us, no matter our differences, has something unique about them that makes them who they are. I believe that everyone has a voice and that finding that voice is a great challenge and a great opportunity.

I realize there may be some words used in the story you just read that you don't understand. For this reason, a glossary follows which contains brief definitions of some of these words. I hope you find this useful, and I encourage you to go back and read the story again for an even better understanding after you have reviewed the meaning of these words.

Glossary

appeased – satisfied when hostile or demanding

compulsion – the action or state of forcing or being forced to do something, constraint

curtailed – cut short

dispelled – scattered, driven off

dole – money, food, etc., given to the unemployed

edict – decree, law

engender – bring into being

faction – group promoting its own interests

leviathan – of immense size and power

levies – taxes, fees or fines, or the act of imposing taxes, fees or fines

pillager – a person who steals things from a place or region, especially in war, using violence

pilfered – stolen, stolen stealthily in small amounts and often again and again

recanted – retracted, renounced

renowned – of great reputation

shill – an accomplice of a hawker, gambler, or swindler who acts as an enthusiastic customer to entice or encourage others

subsistence – the condition of remaining in existence

tenet – doctrine accepted as truth

trove – a store of valuable or delightful things

Printed in the USA
CPSIA information can be obtained
at www.ICGtesting.com
LVHW061741071023
760448LV00017B/208